I0006976

PRODUCTIVE DEVOPS

Your Complete Handbook on Building a Dependable, Agile and Secure Organization

Austin Young

TABLE OF CONTENT

Introduction

For years, operations and development were done by separate teams. Developers created the code, while operators integrated and deployed the code. Each team worked separately from the other team, caused by inadequate communication between them. DevOps helped to bridge that gap, with the objective of developing dependable high-quality software faster while bringing about better collaboration and communication between teams.

DevOps combines both development and operations. DevOps is an approach with the goal of unifying operations (integration and deployment), quality assurance and development into one continual group of processes. However, DevOps is more than just a group of processes rather, it is more of a philosophy or culture that nurtures cross-functional team collaboration and communication. It defines available methods of increasing processes through which a concept (such as a defect fix or an extra application module) can progress from development and deploy into production to offer value to the user. For these processes to be successful, both the operations and development teams must communicate often and proceed towards their tasks with affinity for other team members. DevOps aims to:

- Enhance mean time-to-delivery.
- Reduce lead-time between resolutions.
- Reduce the frequency of failure of new releases.
- Realize faster time-to-market.
- Enhance deployment rate.

Chapter 1

History

DevOps evolved from different software development methodologies. Starting from the inefficient traditional Waterfall model, which evolved into Agile methodology, where software development is in short iterations of about two weeks. Having such short sprints helped the developers work on getting client responses and combining it together with defect resolutions in the next release. Even though this approach was beneficial to developers, it was not the same for operators, as they could not adjust to the speed of agile implementations. Absence of teamwork between operators and developers also affected the releases and development flows. DevOps practice arose out of this requirement for faster releases and improved collaboration.

DevOps methodology extend agile development process by further simplifying the progression of software changes through the build, test, deploy and delivery phases, while enabling cross-functional teams with complete accountability of applications from development to production.

DevOps Concepts and Lifecycle

The delivery cycle of DevOps includes preparation, development, analysis, deployment, release and supervision, with dynamic collaboration between team members. Below is the DevOps lifecycle:

- **Continuous Development**
  In this phase of the DevOps lifecycle, software is continually developed. Different from the Waterfall model, developers commit code in small amounts several times a day for easy testing. Here, we have coding and building, plus the utilization of such tools like SVN and GIT for version

control, and tools such as Gradle and Maven for build automation.

- **Continuous Testing**

  This type of automated testing examines additional code immediately it is added to the repository. The developers are alerted of all possible errors and outputs to help them know the exact set of codes that caused the issue. Continuous testing helps to unite the work of the operators, users and developers. It also aids leaders to grow the scope of what they are comfortable with, when planning software release. Please note that continuous testing is different from automated testing. Continuous testing enables companies to evaluate the threats related with all possible releases once it is committed, whereas automated testing deals with testing more than one possible release simultaneously, making the reason for the problem not too clear. Examples of well-known tools include *Junit* and *Selenium*. There are multiple benefits to continuous testing, these include: reduced risk, enhanced security, better quality and speed of code development, and increased application performance.

- **Continuous Integration**

  This is the process of rapidly merging newly created code to the source code. Because there is continual development, the modified code must be merged continually and effortlessly, to reveal modifications to the end users. The modified code should contain no errors, to make it easy for quick testing. An example of a popular continuous testing tool is *Jenkins*. With Jenkins, a team member can get the most recent code changes from GIT repository and generate a build that can be sent to test or development environment. Jenkins can be configured to start a build automatically or manually, once there is a modification in the repository.

- **Continuous Delivery**
This is a continuation of the continuous integration phase. This involves getting all the modifications into production-like system rapidly and securely in a maintainable manner, and making certain that the applications work as it should via meticulous automated testing. Since each change is sent to a production-like system utilizing automation, there is an assurance that the software can be sent to production whenever the business needs it.

- **Continuous Deployment**

  This is the subsequent stage of continuous delivery, as all modifications that successfully passes the automated tests are automatically sent to production. Since there is constant deployment of new code, need for configuration management tools arises. Some well-known tools are *Ansible, Chef* and *Puppet.*

- **Continuous Monitoring**

  The last phase of the DevOps lifecycle is focused on the evaluation of the entire cycle. The objective of the evaluation is to identify the difficult parts of a procedure and scrutinize the response from the users and team, to report current defects and increase the product's operation. Continuous monitoring includes the involvement of the Operations team who will observe the user actions for defects or any inappropriate system performance. This can similarly be accomplished through the usage of exclusive monitoring tools, to constantly observe the system performance and pinpoint problems. Examples of well-known tools include *Sensu*, *NewRelic*, *Nagios*, and *Splunk*. These tools aid in monitoring the servers and the application thoroughly, to review the condition of the system preemptively. They can also minimize the cost of IT support, multiply the dependability of the system and enhance productivity. When critical problems are identified, the development team should be notified for them to resolve that in the continuous development phase.

DevOps Tools

The core aim to execute DevOps is to enhance the integration procedure and delivery pipeline by automating these events. Consequently, the product will have a shorter time-to-market. To accomplish this automated delivery pipeline, the company should obtain certain tools rather than developing them from scratch.

Presently, existing DevOps tools covers practically every phase of continuous delivery, beginning from continuous integration and stopping with deployment and containerization. Although custom scripts are still used to automate some processes, most DevOps engineers utilize available open source software. Below are the categories for DevOps tools:

- **Build and deploy**

  The tools in this category can be utilized to automatically build and deploy software all through the DevOps lifecycle. In an operational DevOps process, software deployments are dependable, anticipated and recurrent. Deployment tools are vital to realizing this. Continuous delivery makes sure that software can be deployed to production whenever it is needed, to enhance time-to-market and reduce risks. Some popular tools include *SonarQube, Jenkins, XebiaLabs*, and *IBM uDeploy*.

- **Automated testing**

  The tools in this category can deliver improved performance, consistent products and automated testing services. The main aim here though would be to ensure end-to-end automation. Automated testing tools are charged with validating the quality of the code before completing the build. The faster the feedback cycle works, the better the quality, and the faster the team reaches the desired state. Some popular tools include *Water* and *Selenium*.

- **Source/version control**
  The tools in this category can monitor software release versions, either automatically or manually, and are somewhat associated with change management tools. This involves assigning numbers to the different release versions, monitoring the configuration and any form of dependencies in the development environment, for example the required virtual or physical server, the details of the operating system, and/or the

version, brand or type of database. Some popular tools include *Subversion* and *GIT*.

- **Change/configuration management**
  The tools in this category can be used to log and track any software, data or configuration changes, and allocate the platforms required to deploy the software. The utilization of these tools makes sure that the system can return to a stable state, regardless of any event that takes place. Without configuration tools, it would not be possible to attain any kind of stability at scale or administer preferred state norms. Treat infrastructure no different from code that can be configured and provisioned in a repeatable way. Preventing configuration drift through systems will conserve precious time and resolve the

challenges caused by an application working properly in one system but failing in another system. Some popular tools include *Salt*, *Chef* and *Puppet*.

- **Issue Tracking**
  These tools enhance visibility and responsiveness. Every team should utilize the same issue tracking tool, integrating internal issue tracking information together with those generated by the customer. Some popular tools include *ZenDesk* and *Jira*.

Benefits of DevOps

The main benefits of adopting DevOps cover cultural, business and technical aspects of development. These include

- **Improved internal culture**
  DevOps practices and principles bring about enhanced communication

between team members as well as growth in agility and efficiency. Teams that implement DevOps are regarded to be more cross-skilled and efficient. Team members in a DevOps process, including operators and developers, act as one. Unexpected work is a reality that all teams experience, and it sometimes affect team efficiency. With clear prioritization and recognized procedures, the operators and developers can more excellently handle unexpected work while sustaining focus on expected work. Prioritizing and transitioning unexpected work through various systems and teams is unproductive and diverts from current work. Nonetheless, via proactive retrospection and increased visibility, teams can more successfully expect and share unexpected work.

- **Business benefits**

  While in the DevOps process, a team can respond quickly to change requests from users concerning inserting new components and modifying current features. Consequently, the value-delivery and time-to-market rate increases.

- **Quality and speed**

  DevOps aids in increasing the speed of product release by letting developers resolve system issues in the early phases, encouraging quicker feedback, and presenting continuous delivery. Implementing DevOps, the team can concentrate on the code quality while automating some processes. The team that have the quickest feedback cycle is a team that succeeds. Continuous communication and complete transparency allow DevOps teams to reduce slowdowns and fix problems quicker than in the past. If serious problems are not rapidly fixed, client satisfaction falls. Absence of review cycles and automations hinder the deployment to production, and insufficient issue resolution time destroys team assurance and velocity. Disparate processes and tools slow down momentum, bring about context switching, and increase operational expenses. Via standardized processes and tools, plus automation, teams can increase efficiency and deploy more often with less setbacks. Crucial problems fall through the cracks when there is no open communication, leading to frustration and higher tension among teams. Open communication aids

operators and developers to discuss
about concerns, resolve issues, and
release the deployment pipeline quicker.

Chapter 2

Getting Started with DevOps

Switching to a DevOps perspective can be a puzzling and intimidating prospect, particularly since DevOps mostly entails breaking down silos across Operations and Development; leading to a major change in an organization's outlook, development and management of its infrastructure. DevOps as a whole is a mindset, wherein in an ideal scenario, business stakeholders, system administrators and developers would be able to work together as a single team.

After having reviewed the tools stated previously, checking the team's readiness to embark on this journey is important. To do this, a review of certain aspects is necessary.

- **Determine expected outcome**
  Before the transition process begins, it is important to know what the company

expects from the transition to DevOps. So that there will be better structure and reporting when the company has made progress in the DevOps journey. Below are some of the metrics to put into consideration:

- o The length of time it takes to have a feature fully implemented, from requirements gathering to when it is finally utilized by the customer in production.
- o The length of time it takes to develop a feature after the requirements gathering phase.
- o The length of time it takes from when code is committed to when deployment to production is completed.
- o The length of time it takes to reestablish operations after an outage or incident.

- The frequency of code deployment.
- The rate of failed changes.
- The rate of customer and employee satisfaction.

- **Visualize**

  It is important to have a clear knowledge of the movement of information from development to production and have a defined way to automate that. Visualizing the end-to-end workflow has a variety of benefits, as shown below:
  - Helps in clarifying task assignment, work in progress, and challenges/issues
  - Helps employees in the company to comprehend how their effort adds to the success of a project.
  - Helps to create a collaborative environment as employees work

towards a collective realization of success. This will lead to a reduction in duplicate work, misplaced work and uneven distribution of tasks.

- o Helps to identify waste, which includes any type of re-work that could be avoided, such as bug fixes, incidents or production issues.

- **Automate**

There is need for a strong knowledge of the company goals, team goals and tasks. This will aid to evaluate the backlog and remove details/tasks that have zero chance of been implemented, as well as tasks that offer no value. Focus should be on going through the lifecycle of DevOps on a systematic basis. Starting from Continuous Development all the way to Continuous Monitoring.

- **Set up a formal process**

  The success of DevOps partly relies on a company setting up a formal process while continuously enhancing it. In most cases, this can be any form of agile methodology like Lean Software Development, Kanban, Scrum and so on. Regular standups, team retrospectives and end user presentation are some of the opportunities that can help in enhancing the company's formal process. In addition, another key to success in DevOps centers on how effectively teams can work together. Individuals in a team should work from the same process with similar intention of improvement.

In order to establish efficient and effective teams, team members need to develop a better comprehension of each other and provide their expertise at the same time. This might probably lead to a problem where there are some people that "have more knowledge concerning few aspects" and other people that "have little knowledge of several aspects". Due to this, a balance would need to be established, and can be achieved by having the more knowledgeable team or persons make arrangement for an appropriate time to discuss proficiencies and share knowledge. Some examples of ways this can be carried out include knowledge sharing sessions, training, meetups, pair programming and peer review.

DevOps Best Practices

When looking at DevOps, there are lots of moving parts to examine. There is a huge difference in categories and amount of problem domains when making comparisons. The categories of tools or methods that operation and development team members utilize also differ a lot. The Fundamentals of DevOps has to do with automated deployment and build, automated testing as well as automated provisioning. Simultaneously, there is a necessity for well-documented logs and uninterrupted feedback loop, with a constant flow of information.

- **Adopt a security-first perspective**
  The need for security cannot be overstated. In this era, weaknesses and breaches continue to generate considerable monetary and reputational losses to companies of varying capabilities and sizes. The system for

Continuous Delivery (CD) and Continuous Integration (CI) is a major target for hackers, since it provides access to a company's code repository and authorizations to deploy in multiple environments. It is surely not rare to save authorizations in remote repositories for automation purposes. Due to this, it is advised to use secure internal networks to host corporate systems utilized for CI/CD. Factors to enforce for a more secured system include

- making sure that security is part of the development activities all through the process
- access and identity administrative systems
- robust two-factor authentication
- VPN

- **Break down silos**

  In most companies, it is noticeable that, for years, the information technology teams work in formal silos. In this case, there would be a department developing the application, subsequently the application is handed over to the operations team for integration, and then passed over to the QA team for testing, at the end of which the application then returns to the operations and development team for deployment. The splitting of these tasks leads to a restriction on dynamic collaboration, hence, resulting in problems that may interrupt application deployment. A key viewpoint of DevOps is that support, operations and development employees must work as one daily. Restructuring the teams into DevOps teams that includes all necessary disciplines will help to deliver applications faster, effectively and efficiently.

- **Automate**

  Even though a progressive strategy to automation seems perfect, companies switching from manual to automated approach sometimes notice difficulty when determining the initial process to automate. For instance, it is advantageous to automate the procedure for code compilation first. This is because developers have to commit code every day; thus, it is reasonable to carry out automated smoke tests. In order to minimize the workload on developers, automating unit tests first are most common. Accordingly, there is automated functional testing, accompanied by User Interface (UI) testing. Compared to UI tests that have more recurrent changes, functional tests do not usually need frequent modifications in the automation script. The key point is to consider every potential dependency and appraise their capability to prioritize automation reasonably.

When tried and productive practices are in order, manually operating the build of environments for new applications increases a risk that important requirements or elements will be overlooked or steadily reversed to legacy implementations. Stopping development to handle a situation that ought to have been automated, can decline the process of deployment to production.

- **Select proficient tools that align with company's DevOps approach**

Proper tools are essential when adopting DevOps. It is imperative for companies to ensure that all the tools used by the teams are integrated. Discussed below are some of the best practices for selecting tools when implementing DevOps:

- o **Know the team's shared and collaboration tools plan**
  DevOps teams should create a shared tools plan that allows for collaboration all through development, testing and deployment. Developing a shared tools plan may not necessarily lead to immediate tool selection, it shows a plan accepted by every team member and that is reflective of the company's aim for DevOps. A shared DevOps tools plan should conform to a shared collection of

objectives while delivering unified integration and collaboration between tools. This plan should include DevOps

- CloudOps tools and continuous operations
- Continuous deployment tools
- Continuous testing tools
- Continuous integration tools
- Continuous development tools
- Collaboration and communications planning
- Processes

o **Record all requests**
All emergency changes or tasks, requests for updated or new software should take place within

the DevOps process. With DevOps, it is possible to automate change requests acceptance gotten either from other sections of the teams or from the business.

o **Automate with Kanban**
Kanban is a framework that executes agile software development, matching the team's capability to the quantity of work in progress. It offers additional adaptable planning opportunities, transparency, clear focus, and quicker productivity all through the development cycle. Kanban tools present the capacity to visualize today's work or every other item in reference with each other. Additionally, the tools restrict the quantity of work in

progress, aiding in balancing flow-based methodologies. Kanban tools improves flow, such that, after the completion of a certain work item, the subsequent top item in the backlog gets propelled to development.

- o **Log metrics**
  Companies should choose tools, both manual and automated, that can aid in comprehending the efficiency of DevOps processes, and to decide if those tools are working as expected. Those tools can carry out a variety of operations. The initial step is to outline the metrics needed for the DevOps process, like number of testing errors found and rate of deployment. The other step is to

outline the automated procedure for fixing concerns without human involvement. For instance, the problems with scaling software automatically on cloud-based infrastructures.

- o **Execute tooling for test data automation**

  Test data automation involves much more than automated testing; it is the ability to implement standard testing procedures to guarantee code quality, data integrity as well as the quality of the entire solution. In a DevOps process, testing must be continuous. The insertion of data and code into the process means that the code will be in a sandbox, test data allocated to the application, and numerous tests run. When this is finished, the code is either automatically promoted in the DevOps process, or sent back to developers for rework.

o **Carry out acceptance tests**
Acceptance tests should be carried out on each deployment, and this includes stages of recognition for the test suites, data, applications and infrastructure. The tool set chosen should be able to certify that the acceptance tests meets the selected criteria. There is no fixed test format and criteria set, as changes might need to be made at any time by either operations or development. As applications progress gradually, additional

requirements will be
implemented, and tests carried out
against the changes. For example,
attending to performance issues to
make sure that the company meets
service-level agreements, or
testing modifications to
compliance issues related to
safeguarding some forms of data.

o **Ensure continuous feedback**
There is a need for feedback loops
to automate interaction between
tests supported by the selected
DevOps tools and tests that
identify problems. The correct tool
must identify the problem by
using either automated or manual
systems. After which, the tool can
tag the problem with the artifact
so the operators or developers can

see where it happened, why it happened, and what happened. The DevOps tool need to aid in outlining a sequence of communications, having every human user and automated systems in the loop. This involves a methodology to fix the issue in collaboration with all team members, a list of any extra technology or code required and an agreement regarding the form of action to take. When deploying to production, the tool should help in generating reports containing information on if the agreed upon solution successfully completed automated operations, automated deployment and automated testing.

- **Continuous deployment and frequent releases**

  According to a report by Puppet Lab, IT companies that are high-performers rebound from failure about a hundred and sixty-eight times sooner, and have sixty times lesser failures than lower-performing companies have. These high-performing companies also release thirty times more often, while having two hundred times shorter lead times. Growth in the deployment frequency should be an important goal for any company embarking on the DevOps journey. For this, some agile development techniques could help, for instance Scrum, pair programming, and test-driven development. These techniques and technology are for accomplishing goals such as improved support, enhanced code quality and faster deployment.

For regular releases to take place, the application should be in a release-ready format and tested in an environment that is like that of Production. Some aspects to put into consideration here are:

- o **A/B testing**: is a method of directing a small number of users to a new feature under distinct conditions. It is mostly a way to carry out business decisions based on statistics instead of a deployment tactic. Nonetheless, there is a relationship here since it executes by inputting additional functionality to a canary deployment. Here, there is a comparison of features in an application to determine usability or performance. The feature that performs better gets rolled out. The conditions needed to allocate traffic amongst the versions are language, technology support (operating system, screen size, browser version etc.), geolocation, query parameters and through browser cookie. The benefit of this method involves having complete control over the distribution of traffic and having various versions run in parallel. The drawbacks of this method involve difficulty with troubleshooting errors for a specific session, thus making distributed tracing compulsory, as this method also demands smart load balancer.

- Blue-green deployment: is a method that minimizes risk and interruption by managing two similar production environments known as Blue and Green. At whatever time, there would only be one environment live, and this environment would attend to every production traffic. To have a better picture, Blue is the presently live environment, while Green is idle. During preparation for a new release, the last phase of testing and deployment occurs in the environment that is not currently live (Green). After carrying out deployment and testing in the not live environment, there would be a switch in the router to that environment with the most recent releases (Green). If an unexpected event occurs because of the deployment, a rollback to the previous versions can be done by switching to the previous environment (Blue). The advantages of this method involve avoiding issues with versioning as the whole application state is modified at once, as well as having instant rollback/rollout. The disadvantages of this method include the difficulty of managing stateful applications, needs appropriate testing of the whole application before deployment to production, and the method is expensive since it entails dual resources.

In blue-green deployment, similar database backend or persistence layer for both environments are used. Keeping data synchronized is important, however, a mirrored database can aid in accomplishing that. A company can choose to utilize the main database in the blue environment for write operations, and utilize the ancillary database in the green environment for read operations. Whenever there is a failover from the blue environment to the green environment, a switch over from main to ancillary will occur. The databases can be in two-way replication, just in case there is need to write data during testing in green environment. For seamless switching between the blue and green environments, below are the best practices:

- **Select load balancing instead of DNS Switching**

  During environment switch, the domain ultimately points to separate servers. Altering the DNS management interface is not ideal, since the browsers can take a while to acquire the new IP address. Thus, leading to a long traffic tail to your former environment. This suggests that there is no full control over the traffic routing, as the previous environment will still serve several users. Load balancers will help to have the servers set up

instantaneously, with no
dependence on the DNS
process. The DNS record
will reference the load
balancer. This way there is
a surety that traffic routes
to the correct environment.

- **Implement a
  continuous update**
  There might be a downtime
  when moving servers
  between versions.
  Implementing a rolling
  update will prevent this.
  Rather than switching all
  the servers at one go,
  working with an integrated
  environment is the way to
  go. Retirement of old
  servers and addition of new
  servers should be done

one-by-one, repeatedly, until the process is complete. It is important to note that there is a need to utilize connection depletion on the load balancers for finalization of requests on the old server before it is disengaged.

- **Track alerts**
Getting rid of defects before they get to production is key, and that is why proper monitoring must be in place for not only the production environment, but for the non-production environment as well. There should be an appropriate system in place to set up